MW00570646

ANGEL DEVOTION PRAYERBOOK

Compiled by Luis Valverde

ANGEL DEVOTION PRAYERBOOK
Compiled by Luis Valverde

Edited by L.C. Fiore
Cover/Text Design and Typesetting by Patricia A. Lynch

Front Cover Photo Credit:
Scala/Ministero per i Beni e le Attività culturali/Art Resource, NY

For permission to reprint the artwork and prayers that appear in this book, we are grateful for the copyright owners listed on pages 45-49, whose generosity and cooperation made this book possible. The "Credits and Permissions" section represents an extension of the copyright page.

Scripture quotes are from the *New Revised Standard Version of the Bible*, copyright © 1989 by the Division of Christian Education of the National Council of the Churches of Christ in the USA. All rights reserved. Used with permission.

Copyright © 2012 by Luis Valverde

Published by ACTA Publications, 4848 N. Clark Street, Chicago, IL 60640-4711, (800) 397-2282, www.actapublications.com.

All rights reserved. No part of this publication may be reproduced or transmitted in any form or by any means, electronic or mechanical, including photocopying and recording, or by any information storage and retrieval system, including the Internet, without permission from the publisher. Permission is hereby given to use short excerpts with proper citation in reviews, newsletters, church bulletins, class handouts, and scholarly papers.

ISBN: 978-0-87946-482-0
Printed in the United States of America by Total Printing Systems
Year: 20 19 18 17 16 15 14 13 12
Printing: 10 9 8 7 6 5 4 3 2 First

♻ Black text printed on 30% post-consumer recycled paper

CONTENTS

ANGEL DEVOTION

*From infancy to death, human life is surrounded
by their watchful care and intercession.*

Catechism of the Catholic Church

Why pray to angels? Why not just pray to God directly, in
the name of Jesus, as he taught us? In the Roman Catholic
tradition, at least, the answer lies in the word *intercession*, as in
"intercede for us" with God. For some reason, we often feel more
comfortable praying to the mother of Jesus, or to one of the saints
that the church has canonized, or even to loved ones who have
died and we are sure now enjoy God's presence in a special and
real way, even though they are now spirits.

So it is not difficult for us to also have devotion to angelic beings
who were *always* spirits. After all, they've been around for a lot
longer than human beings have, and they always seem to show up
at really important times. (For example, they brought Abraham the
news that his wife Sarah was pregnant, led the Israelites through
the desert, announced to Mary that she was to be the mother of the
Messiah, let the shepherds in the fields know that Jesus had been
born, and will be battling Satan and his demons during the world's
final conflict.) The word *angel* means "messenger."

We don't really know much about angels. Only three of them—
Michael, Gabriel, and Raphael—are mentioned by name in the
Bible. But the job of all angels seems to be to help protect us,
and so we have also come to believe in our personal "Guardian
Angel." This book has compiled devotional prayers to these four
angels, which can be used to ask for their intercession with God
for us.

- **Michael the Archangel**: *Michael* means "Who is like God?" He is mentioned by name in Daniel 12:1 and Revelation 12:7 and is generally thought to be the leader of the angelic forces against the forces of evil. Therefore he is asked to help us have courage, resist temptation, and remain safe in dangerous situations.

- **Gabriel the Archangel**: *Gabriel* means "God is my strength." He is mentioned by name in Daniel 8:16; 9:21; and of course in Luke 1:19, 26 and is the messenger of God's will to Daniel, Zechariah, Mary, and probably others. Therefore he is asked to help us clear up confusion, achieve wisdom, make decisions, take action, communicate effectively, and raise children.

- **Raphael the Archangel**: *Raphael* means "God heals." He is mentioned by name in the entire book of Tobit, where in disguise he helps Tobit, his son Tobias, and Tobias' wife Sarah get their lives straightened out, including curing Tobit's blindness. Therefore he is asked to help with physical, mental, and emotional illness; addiction; safe travel; and the health of animals and the environment.

- **Our Guardian Angel**: Angels are mentioned as our *guardians* in Exodus 32:34, Psalm 91:11, Tobit 5:22, and Matthew 18:10, where Jesus says "Take care that you do not despise one of these little ones; for, I tell you, in heaven their angels continually see the face of my Father in heaven." Therefore our Guardian Angel is asked to help with protection (especially of children), comfort, love, faith, and the trials and tribulations of daily life.

The prayers in this book are meant to be used for both personal and group devotion. They can be said before or after the recitation of the Rosary, before or after Mass, before going to bed or around the dinner table, on retreats, in schools, with prayer groups, and in conjunction with *novenas*, which are nine repetitions of any prayer or set of prayers for a particular cause.

SAINT MICHAEL THE ARCHANGEL

Photo Credit: Scala/Art Resource, NY

Michael the Archangel defeating Satan

Prayer to Saint Michael

O glorious Archangel Saint Michael, prince of the heavenly host, be our defense in the terrible warfare which we carry on against principalities and powers, against the rulers of this world of darkness, spirits of evil. Come to the aid of the human race, whom God created immortal, made in His own image and likeness, and redeemed at a great price from the tyranny of the Devil. Fight this day the battle of the Lord, together with the holy angels, as already thou hast fought the leader of the proud angels, Lucifer, and his apostate host, who were powerless to resist thee, nor was there place for them any longer in Heaven. That cruel, that ancient serpent, who is called the Devil or Satan, who seduces the whole world, was cast into the abyss with his angels. Behold this primeval enemy and slayer of men has taken courage. Transformed into an angel of light, he wanders about with all the multitude of wicked spirits, invading the earth in order to blot out the name of God and of His Christ, to seize upon, slay, and cast into eternal perdition souls destined for the crown of eternal glory.

This wicked dragon pours out, as a most impure flood, the venom of his malice on men of depraved mind and corrupt heart, the spirit of lying, of impiety, of blasphemy, and the pestilent breath of impurity, and of every vice and iniquity. These most crafty enemies have filled and inebriated with gall and bitterness the Church, the spouse of the immaculate Lamb, and have laid impious hands on her most sacred possessions. In the Holy Place itself, where has been set up the See of the most holy Peter and the Chair of Truth for the light of the world, they have raised the throne of their abominable impiety, with the iniquitous design that when the pastor has been struck, the sheep may be scattered.

Arise then, O invincible prince, bring help against the attacks of the lost spirits to the people of God, and give them the victory. They venerate thee as their protector and patron; in thee holy Church glories as her defense against the malicious power of Hell; to thee has God entrusted the souls of men to be established in heavenly beatitude. Oh, pray to the God of peace that He may put Satan under our feet, so far conquered that he may no longer be able to hold us in captivity and harm the Church. Offer our prayers in the sight of the Most High, so that they may quickly conciliate the mercies of the Lord; and beating down the dragon, the ancient serpent, who is the Devil and Satan, do thou again make him captive in the abyss, that he may no longer seduce the nations. Amen.

V. Behold the Cross of the Lord; be scattered ye hostile powers.

R. The lion of the tribe of Judah has conquered,

    the root of David.

V. Let thy mercies be upon us, O Lord.

R. As we have hoped in thee.

V. O Lord, hear my prayer.

R. And let my cry come unto thee.

Let us pray.

O God, the Father of our Lord Jesus Christ, we call upon thy holy name, and as suppliants we implore thy clemency, that by the intercession of Mary, ever Virgin immaculate and our Mother, and of the glorious Archangel Saint Michael, thou wouldst deign to help us against Satan and all other unclean spirits, who wander about the world for the injury of the human race and the ruin of souls. Amen.

Saint Michael Prayer (Shortened Version)

Saint Michael, the Archangel, defend us in battle; be our protection against the wickedness and snares of the Devil. May God rebuke him, we humbly pray: and do thou, O prince of the heavenly host, by the power of God, cast into Hell Satan and all wicked spirits who roam through the world, seeking the ruin of souls. Amen.

Prayer for Help against Spiritual Enemies

Glorious Saint Michael, prince of the heavenly hosts, who stands always ready to give assistance to the people of God; who didst fight with the dragon, the old serpent, and didst cast him out of Heaven, and now valiantly defends the Church of God that the gates of Hell may never prevail against her, I earnestly entreat you to assist me also, in the painful and dangerous conflict which I have to sustain against the same formidable foe. Be with me, O mighty prince! That I may courageously fight and wholly vanquish that proud spirit, whom though cast, by the Divine Power, so gloriously overthrown, and whom our powerful King, Jesus Christ, has, in our nature, so completely overcome; to the end that having triumphed over the enemy of my salvation, I may with thee and the holy angels, praise the clemency of God who, having refused mercy to the rebellious angels after their fall, has granted repentance and forgiveness to the fallen human race. Amen.

NOVENA TO SAINT MICHAEL

V. O God, come to my assistance.
R. O Lord, make haste to help me.

Glory be to the Father, etc.

Saint Michael the Archangel, loyal champion of God and His people, I turn to you with confidence and seek your powerful intercession. For the love of God, who made you so glorious in grace and power, and for the love of the Mother of Jesus, the Queen of the Angels, be pleased to hear my prayer. You know the value of my soul in the eyes of God. May no stain of evil ever disfigure its beauty. Help me to conquer the evil spirit who tempts me. I desire to imitate your loyalty to God and Holy Mother Church and your great love for God and people. And since you are God's messenger for the care of His people, I entrust to you this special request: (*Mention your request*).

Saint Michael, since you are, by the will of the Creator, the powerful intercessor of Christians, I have great confidence in your prayers. I earnestly trust that if it is God's holy will my petition will be granted.

Pray for me, Saint Michael, and also for those I love. Protect us in all dangers of body and soul. Help us in our daily needs. Through your powerful intercession, may we live a holy life, die a happy death, and reach Heaven where we may praise and love God with you forever. Amen.

LITANY OF SAINT MICHAEL

Lord, have mercy.
Christ, have mercy.
Lord, have mercy.
Christ, hear us.
Christ, graciously hear us.
God, the Father of Heaven, have mercy on us.
God, the Son, the Redeemer of the world, have mercy on us.
God, the Holy Ghost, have mercy on us.
Holy Trinity, one God, have mercy on us.
Holy Mary, Queen of Angels, pray for us.
Saint Michael, pray for us.
Holy Mary, Queen of Angels, pray for us.
Saint Michael, pray for us.
Saint Michael, filled with the wisdom of God, pray for us.
Saint Michael, perfect adorer of the incarnate Word, pray for us.
Saint Michael, crowned with honor and glory, pray for us.
Saint Michael, most powerful prince of the armies of the Lord,
    pray for us.
Saint Michael, standard-bearer of the Most Holy Trinity,
    pray for us.
Saint Michael, victor over Satan, pray for us.
Saint Michael, guardian of Paradise, pray for us.
Saint Michael, guide and comforter of the people of Israel,
    pray for us.
Saint Michael, splendor and fortress of the Church Militant,
    pray for us.
Saint Michael, honor and joy of the Church Triumphant,
    pray for us.
Saint Michael, light of angels, pray for us.
Saint Michael, bulwark of orthodox believers, pray for us.

Saint Michael, strength of those who fight under the standard of the Cross, pray for us.

Saint Michael, light and confidence of souls at the hour of death, pray for us.

Saint Michael, our most sure aid, pray for us.

Saint Michael, our help in all adversities, pray for us.

Saint Michael, herald of the Everlasting Sentence, pray for us.

Saint Michael, consoler of souls detained in the flames of Purgatory, pray for us.

Thou whom the Lord has charged to receive souls after death, pray for us.

Saint Michael, our prince, pray for us.

Saint Michael, our advocate, pray for us.

Lamb of God, who takest away the sins of the world, spare us, O Lord.

Lamb of God, who takest away the sins of the world, graciously hear us O Lord.

Lamb of God, who takest away the sins of the world, have mercy on us.

Christ hear us.

Christ, graciously hear us.

V. Pray for us, O glorious Saint Michael, Prince of the Church of Jesus Christ.

R. That we may be made worthy of His promises.

Let us pray.

Sanctify us, we beseech thee, O Lord, with thy holy blessing, and grant us, by the intercession of Saint Michael, that wisdom which teaches us to lay up treasures in Heaven by exchanging the goods of this world for those of eternity, thou who livest and reignest, world without end. Amen.

THE CHAPLET OF SAINT MICHAEL

V. O God, come to my assistance.
R. O Lord, make haste to help me.

Glory be to the Father, etc.

Say one Our Father and three Hail Marys after each of the following nine salutations in honor of the nine choirs of angels.

1. By the intercession of Saint Michael and the celestial Choir of Seraphim, may the Lord make us worthy to burn with the fire of perfect charity. Amen.

2. By the intercession of Saint Michael and the celestial Choir of Cherubim, may the Lord grant us the grace to leave the ways of sin and run in the paths of Christian perfection. Amen.

3. By the intercession of Saint Michael and the celestial Choir of Thrones, may the Lord infuse into our hearts a true and sincere spirit of humility. Amen.

4. By the intercession of Saint Michael and the celestial Choir of Dominations, may the Lord give us grace to govern our senses and overcome any unruly passions. Amen.

5. By the intercession of Saint Michael and the celestial Choir of Virtues, may the Lord preserve us from evil and falling into temptation. Amen.

6. By the intercession of Saint Michael and the celestial Choir of Powers, may the Lord protect our souls against the snares and temptations of the Devil. Amen.

7. By the intercession of Saint Michael and the celestial Choir of Principalities, may God fill our souls with a true spirit of obedience. Amen.

8. By the intercession of Saint Michael and the celestial Choir of Archangels, may the Lord give us perseverance in faith and in all good works in order that we may attain the glory of Heaven. Amen.

9. By the intercession of Saint Michael and the celestial Choir of Angels may the Lord grant us to be protected by them in this mortal life and conducted in the life to come to Heaven. Amen.

Say one Our Father in honor of each of the following leading angels: Saint Michael, Saint Gabriel, Saint Raphael, and our Guardian Angel.

Concluding prayers:

O glorious prince Saint Michael, chief and commander of the heavenly hosts, guardian of souls, vanquisher of rebel spirits, servant in the house of the Divine King and our admirable conductor, you who shine with excellence and superhuman virtue deliver us from all evil, who turn to you with confidence and enable us by your gracious protection to serve God more and more faithfully every day.

Pray for us, O glorious Saint Michael, prince of the Church of Jesus Christ, that we may be made worthy of his promises.

Almighty and everlasting God, who, by a prodigy of goodness and a merciful desire for the salvation of all human beings, has appointed the most glorious Archangel Saint Michael prince of your Church, make us worthy, we ask you, to be delivered from all our enemies, that none of them may harass us at the hour of death, but that we may be conducted by him into your Presence. This we ask through the merits of Jesus Christ our Lord. Amen.

SAINT GABRIEL THE ARCHANGEL

Photo Credit: Scala/Art Resource, NY

*Gabriel the Archangel telling Mary
that she has been chosen by God*

Prayer to Saint Gabriel for Intercession

O blessed Archangel Gabriel, we beseech thee, do thou intercede for us at the throne of divine mercy in our present necessities, that as thou didst announce to Mary the mystery of the Incarnation, so through thy prayers and patronage in Heaven we may obtain the benefits of the same, and sing the praise of God forever in the land of the living. Amen.

Prayer to Saint Gabriel for Others

O loving messenger of the Incarnation, descend upon all those for whom I wish peace and happiness. Spread your wings over the cradles of the newborn babes, O you who announced the coming of the infant Jesus.

Give to the young a lily petal from the virginal scepter in your hand; cause the "Ave Maria" to re-echo in all hearts that they may find grace and joy through Mary.

Finally, recall the sublime words spoken on the day of the Annunciation—"Nothing is impossible with God, " and repeat them in hours of trial—to all I love—that their confidence in Our Lord may be reanimated, when all human help fails. Amen.

NOVENA PRAYER TO SAINT GABRIEL

V. O God, come to my assistance.
R. O Lord, make haste to help me.

Glory be to the Father, etc.

Saint Gabriel the Archangel, I venerate you as the Angel of the Incarnation, because God specially appointed you to bear the messages concerning the God-Man to Daniel, Zechariah, and the Blessed Virgin Mary. Give me a very tender and devoted love for the incarnate Word and his Blessed Mother more like your own.

I venerate you also as the "Strength from God" because you are the giver of God's strength, consoler and comforter chosen to strengthen God's faithful and teach them important truths. I ask for the grace of a special power of the will to strive for holiness of life. Steady my resolutions; renew my courage; comfort and console me in the problems, trials, and sufferings of daily living, as you consoled our savior in his agony and Mary in her sorrows and Joseph in his trials.

I put my confidence in you. Saint Gabriel I ask you especially for this favor: (*mention your request*).

Through your earnest love for the Son of God made man and for his Blessed Mother I beg of you, intercede for me that my request may be granted, if it be God's holy will.

Pray for us, Saint Gabriel the Archangel, that we may be worthy of the promises of Christ. Amen.

LITANY OF SAINT GABRIEL

Lord, have mercy on us.
Christ, have mercy on us.
Lord, have mercy on us.
Christ, hear us.
Christ, graciously hear us.
God the Father of Heaven, have mercy on us.
God the Son, Redeemer of the world, have mercy on us.
God the Holy Ghost, have mercy on us.
Holy Trinity, One God, have mercy on us.
Holy Mary, Queen of Angels, pray for us.
Saint Gabriel, glorious archangel, pray for us.
Saint Gabriel, strength of God, pray for us.
Saint Gabriel, who standest before the throne of God, pray for us.
Saint Gabriel, model of prayer, pray for us.
Saint Gabriel, herald of the Incarnation, pray for us.
Saint Gabriel, who revealed the glories of Mary, pray for us.
Saint Gabriel, prince of Heaven, pray for us.
Saint Gabriel, ambassador of the Most High, pray for us.
Saint Gabriel, guardian of the Immaculate Virgin, pray for us.
Saint Gabriel, who didst foretell the greatness of Jesus, pray for us.
Saint Gabriel, peace and light of souls, pray for us.
Saint Gabriel, scourge of unbelievers, pray for us.
Saint Gabriel, admirable teacher, pray for us.
Saint Gabriel, strength of the just, pray for us.
Saint Gabriel, protector of the faithful, pray for us.
Saint Gabriel, first adorer of the Divine Word, pray for us.
Saint Gabriel, defender of the Faith, pray for us.
Saint Gabriel, zealous for the honor of Jesus Christ, pray for us.
Saint Gabriel, whom the Scriptures praise as the angel sent by
    God to Mary, the Virgin, pray for us.

Lamb of God, who takest away the sins of the world,
   spare us, O Lord.
Lamb of God, who takest away the sins of the world,
   graciously hear us, O Lord.
Lamb of God, who takest away the sins of the world,
   have mercy on us.

Christ, hear us.
Christ, graciously hear us.

V. Pray for us, blessed Archangel Gabriel,
R. That we may be made worthy of the promises of Jesus Christ.

Let us pray.

O blessed Archangel Gabriel, we beseech thee, do thou intercede
for us at the throne of Divine Mercy in our present necessities,
that as thou didst announce to Mary the mystery of the Incarnation, so through thy prayers and patronage in Heaven, we may
obtain the benefits of the same, and sing the praise of God forever
in the land of the living. Amen.

Chaplet of Saint Gabriel

The Chaplet of Saint Gabriel has a large medal, three small beads, a small medal at the "Y" joint, followed by three sets of eleven beads, each set being separated by a single bead. (There are two of them, often a different size or color from the others.) The three sets of eleven beads honor the 33 years of our Savior's life. The two joining beads honor the divinity and the humanity of the Lord Jesus.

Begin with the following prayer:

First Bead

"Heavenly Father, through the salutation of the Archangel Gabriel, may we honor the Incarnation of your divine son."

Second Bead

"Mother of our savior, may we strive always to imitate your holy virtues and to respond to our Father. Be it done unto me according to thy Word."

Third Bead

"Archangel Gabriel, please praise our Father for the gift of His son praying, one day, by His grace, we may all be one."

On each of the beads in the sets of eleven, you say:

"Hail, full of grace, the Lord is with thee: Blessed art thou among women."

On the two beads that separate each set, you say:

"Behold thou shalt conceive in thy womb, and shalt bring forth a son: and thou shalt call his name Jesus."

SAINT RAPHAEL THE ARCHANGEL

Photo Credit: Scala/Art Resource, NY

*Raphael the Archangel preparing to accompany Tobias
on his journey as Tobit gives his blessing*

Prayer to Saint Raphael the Archangel

O glorious Archangel, Saint Raphael, great prince of the heavenly court, illustrious for your gifts of wisdom and grace, guide of those who journey by land or sea, consoler of the afflicted, and refuge of sinners; I beg you to assist me in all my needs and in all the sufferings of this life, as once you helped the young Tobias on his travels. And because you are the medicine of God, I humbly pray you to heal the many infirmities of my soul, and the ills which afflict my body, if it be for my greater good. I specially ask of you an angelic purity which may fit me to be the temple of the Holy Spirit. Amen.

Prayer to Saint Raphael for a Happy Meeting

O Raphael, lead us toward those we are waiting for, those who are waiting for us! Raphael, angel of happy meetings, lead us by the hand toward those we are looking for! May all our movements be guided by your light and transfigured with your joy.

Angel guide of Tobias, lay the request we now address to you at the feet of Him on whose unveiled face you are privileged to gaze. Lonely and tired, crushed by the separations and sorrows of earth, we feel the need of calling you and of pleading for the protection of your wings, so that we may not be as strangers in the province of joy, all ignorant of the concerns of our country. Remember the weak, you who are strong, you whose home lies beyond the region of thunder, in a land that is always peaceful, always serene and bright with the resplendent glory of God. Amen.

V. O God, come to my assistance.
R. O Lord, make haste to help me.

Glory be to the Father, etc.

The versicle and response are to be repeated every day.

O Christ, splendor of the Father, life and strength of the heart, in the presence of the angels we celebrate you by our prayers and hymns, uniting our voices with their melodious concerts. We praise with reverence all the celestial princes, but especially the Archangel Saint Raphael and faithful companion by whose power the Devil was enchained.

O Christ, king full of goodness, by this guardian remove far from us all the wickedness of the enemy; purify our hearts and our bodies, and by thy sole clemency, introduce us into Paradise. In harmonious concerts let us give thanks to the Father, glory to Jesus Christ and to the comforter, God three in one, living before all ages. Amen.

Hail Mary, etc.

Saint Raphael, pray for us.

The following versicle and prayer are added on the ninth day.

V. Pray for us, Saint Raphael.
R. That we may be made worthy of the promises of Christ.

Let us pray.

O God, who to Tobias, thy servant when on his journey, did give Raphael the Archangel as a companion; grant that we who are also your servants, may likewise be safe-guarded by his watchfulness, and be made strong by his help. May he who we faithfully believe ever to stand before your majesty, offer up our prayers to be blessed by you. This we ask through Jesus Christ, our Lord. Amen.

LITANY OF SAINT RAPHAEL

Lord, have mercy on us.

Christ, have mercy on us.

Lord, have mercy on us.

Christ, hear us.

Christ, graciously hear us.

God the Father of Heaven, have mercy on us.

God the Son, Redeemer of the World, have mercy on us.

God the Holy Ghost, have mercy on us.

Holy Trinity, one God, have mercy on us.

Holy Mary, Queen of Angels, pray for us.

Saint Raphael, pray for us.

Saint Raphael, filled with the mercy of God, pray for us.

Saint Raphael, perfect adorer of the divine Word, pray for us.

Saint Raphael, terror of demons, pray for us.

Saint Raphael, exterminator of vices, pray for us.

Saint Raphael, health of the sick, pray for us.

Saint Raphael, our refuge in all our trials, pray for us.

Saint Raphael, guide of travelers, pray for us.

Saint Raphael, consoler of prisoners, pray for us.

Saint Raphael, joy of the sorrowful, pray for us.

Saint Raphael, filled with zeal for the salvation of souls, pray for us.

Saint Raphael, whose name means "Medicine of God," pray for us.

Saint Raphael, lover of chastity, pray for us.

Saint Raphael, scourge of demons, pray for us.

Saint Raphael, in pest, famine and war, pray for us.

Saint Raphael, angel of peace and prosperity, pray for us.

Saint Raphael, endowed with the grace of healing, pray for us.

Saint Raphael, sure guide in the paths of virtue and
   sanctification, pray for us.

Saint Raphael, help of all those who implore your assistance, pray for us.

Saint Raphael, who wert the guide and consolation of Tobias on his journey, pray for us.

Saint Raphael, whom the Scriptures praise:

"Raphael, the holy angel of the Lord, was sent to cure," pray for us.

Saint Raphael, our advocate, pray for us.

Lamb of God, who takes away the sins of the world, spare us, O Lord.

Lamb of God, who takes away the sins of the world, graciously hear us, O Lord.

Lamb of God, who takes away the sins of the world, have mercy on us.

Christ, hear us.

Christ, graciously hear us.

V. Pray for us, Saint Raphael, to the Lord our God,

R. That we may be made worthy of the promises of Christ.

Let us pray.

Lord Jesus Christ, by the prayer of the Archangel Raphael, grant us the grace to avoid all sin and to persevere in every good work until we reach our heavenly country, thou who lives and reigns world without end. Amen.

CHAPLET OF SAINT RAPHAEL

This chaplet consists of a medal of Saint Raphael, three beads in honor of Mary, Queen of Angels, and nine beads in honor of the nine angelic choirs.

On the medal say:

You are Raphael the healer,
You are Raphael the guide,
You are Raphael the companion,
Ever at human sorrow's side.

On the first beads say three Hail Marys to Mary, Queen of Angels.

On the nine beads say the following prayer, once in honor of each of the nine angelic choirs (angels, archangels, principalities, powers, virtues, dominations, thrones, Cherubim, and Seraphim).

Holy, holy, holy, Lord, God of hosts,
Heaven and Earth are full of your glory.
Glory be to the Father; glory be to the son;
Glory be to the Holy Spirit.

Concluding aspiration:

Saint Raphael, angel of health, of love, of joy and light,
pray for us. Amen.

OUR GUARDIAN ANGEL

Photo Credit: Scala/Ministero per i Beni e le Attività culturali/Art Resource, NY

Guardian Angel leading and protecting a young child

Guardian Angel Prayer

Angel of God, my guardian dear, to whom God's love commits me here, ever this day (night), be at my side, to light and guard, to rule and guide. Amen.

Memorare to Our Guardian Angel

Remember, O holy Angel, that Jesus, the eternal truth, assures us you "rejoice more at the conversion of one sinner than the perseverance of many just." Encouraged thereby, I, the last of creatures, humbly entreat you to receive me as your child, and make me unto you a cause of true joy. Do not, O blessed spirit, reject my petition, but graciously hear and grant it. Amen.

Saint Gertrude's Guardian Angel Prayer

O most holy Angel of God, appointed by Him to be my guardian, I give you thanks for all the benefits which you have ever bestowed on me in body and in soul. I praise and glorify thee that thou condescended to assist me with such patient fidelity, and to defend me against all the assaults of my enemies. Blessed be the hour in which you were assigned me for my guardian, my defender, and my patron. In acknowledgement and return for all thy loving ministries to me from my youth up, I offer thee the infinitely precious and noble heart of Jesus, and firmly purpose to obey thee henceforward, and most faithfully to serve my God. Amen.

RECOMMENDATION TO ONE'S GUARDIAN ANGEL FOR A HAPPY HOUR OF DEATH

My good Angel: I know not when or how I shall die. It is possible I may be carried off suddenly, and that before my last sigh I may be deprived of all intelligence. Yet how many things I would wish to say to God on the threshold of eternity. In the full freedom of my will today, I come to charge you to speak for me at that fearful moment. You will say to Him, then, O my good Angel:

- That I wish to die in the Roman Catholic Apostolic Church in which so many saints since Jesus Christ have died and which is the source of my salvation.

- That I ask the grace of sharing in the infinite merits of my redeemer, and that I desire to die in pressing to my lips to the cross that was bathed in his blood.

- That I detest my sins because they displease Him, and that I pardon through love of Him all my enemies as I wish to be pardoned.

- That I die willingly because He orders it, and that I throw myself with confidence into His adorable heart awaiting all His mercy.

- That in my inexpressible desire to go to Heaven I am disposed to suffer everything it may please His sovereign justice to inflict on me.

- That I love Him before all things, above all things, and for His own sake; that I wish and hope to love Him with the elect, His angels, and the Blessed Mother during all eternity.

Do not refuse, O my angel, to be my interpreter with God, and to protest to Him that these are my sentiments and my will. Amen.

ASPIRATION TO OUR GUARDIAN ANGEL

O my dear Angel Guardian, preserve me from the misfortune of offending God.

NOVENA TO OUR GUARDIAN ANGEL

V. O God, come to my assistance.
R. O Lord, make haste to help me.

Glory be to the Father, etc.

O most faithful companion, appointed by God to be my guardian, and who never leaves my side, how shall I thank you for your faithfulness and love and for the benefits which you have obtained for me?

You watch over me when I sleep; you comfort me when I am sad; you avert the dangers that threaten me and warn me of those to come; you withdraw me from sin and inspire me to good; you exhort me to penance when I fall and reconcile me to God.

I beg you not to leave me. Comfort me in adversity, restrain me in prosperity, defend me in danger, and assist me in temptations, lest at any time I fall beneath them.

Offer up in the sight of the divine majesty my prayers and petitions, and all my works of piety, and help me to persevere in grace until I come to everlasting life. Amen.

Lord, have mercy on us.
Christ, have mercy on us.
Lord, have mercy on us.
Christ, hear us,
Christ, graciously hear us.
God the Father of Heaven, have mercy on us.
God the son, redeemer of the world, have mercy on us.
God the Holy Ghost, have mercy on us,
Holy Trinity, one God, have mercy on us.
Holy Mary, Queen of Angels, pray for us.
Holy Angel, my guardian, pray for us.
Holy Angel, my prince, pray for us.
Holy Angel, my monitor, pray for us.
Holy Angel, my counselor, pray for us.
Holy Angel, my defender, pray for us.
Holy Angel, my steward, pray for us.
Holy Angel, my friend, pray for us.
Holy Angel, my negotiator, pray for us.
Holy Angel, my intercessor, pray for us.
Holy Angel, my patron, pray for us.
Holy Angel, my director, pray for us.
Holy Angel, my ruler, pray for us.
Holy Angel, my protector, pray for us.
Holy Angel, my comforter, pray for us.
Holy Angel, my brother, pray for us.
Holy Angel, my teacher, pray for us.
Holy Angel, my shepherd, pray for us.
Holy Angel, my witness, pray for us.
Holy Angel, my helper, pray for us.
Holy Angel, my watcher, pray for us.

Holy Angel, my conductor, pray for us.

Holy Angel, my preserver, pray for us.

Holy Angel, my instructor, pray for us.

Holy Angel, my enlightener, pray for us.

Lamb of God, who takest away the sins of the world, spare us, O Lord!

Lamb of God, who takest away the sins of the world, graciously hear us, O Lord!

Lamb of God, who takest away the sins of the world, have mercy on us!

Christ, hear us.

Christ graciously hear us.

Lord, have mercy on us.

V. Pray for us, O holy Angel Guardian.

R. That we may be made worthy of the promises of Christ.

Let us pray.

Almighty, everlasting God, who in the counsel of thy ineffable goodness have appointed to all the faithful, from their mother's womb, a special angel guardian of their body and soul; grant, that I may so love and honor him whom you have so mercifully given me, that protected by the bounty of your grace and by his assistance, I may merit to behold, with him and all the angelic host, the glory of your countenance in the heavenly kingdom. Who livest and reignest, world without end. Amen.

Chaplet of the Holy Angels

Recited in the morning:

O my Jesus, I offer this chaplet to your divine heart, that you may render it perfect, thus giving joy to your holy angels, and so they may keep me under their holy protection, above all at the hour of my death to which I invite them with all my heart. Strengthened by their presence, I will await death with joy and be preserved from the assaults of Hell. I beseech you also, dear angels, to visit immediately the souls in Purgatory, especially my parents, my friends, my benefactors; help them so that they will soon be delivered. Do not forget me either after my death. This I beg you with all my heart, through the sacred heart of Jesus and the immaculate heart of Mary, Amen.

- Saint Michael, I recommend the hour of my death to you! Hold the evil one prisoner, so that he may not battle against me and do no harm to my soul—*one Our Father, three Hail Marys.*

- Saint Gabriel, obtain for me from God lively faith, strong hope, ardent charity, and great devotion to the Blessed Sacrament of the altar—*one Our Father, three Hail Marys.*

- Saint Raphael, lead me constantly on the road of virtue and perfection—*one Our Father, three Hail Marys.*

- My holy Guardian Angel, obtain for me divine inspiration and the special grace to be faithful—*one Our Father, three Hail Marys.*

- O ardent Seraphim, obtain for me a burning love for God—*one Our Father, three Hail Marys.*

- O Cherubim, brilliant with light, obtain for me true knowledge of the science of the saints—*one Our Father, three Hail Marys.*

- O admirable thrones, obtain for me peace and tranquility of heart—*one Our Father, three Hail Marys.*

- O exulted dominions, obtain for me victory over all evil thoughts—*one Our Father, three Hail Marys.*

- O invincible powers, obtain for me strength against all evil spirits—*one Our Father, three Hail Marys.*

- O most serene virtues, obtain for me obedience and perfect justice—*one Our Father, three Hail Marys.*

- O principalities, who accomplish prodigies, obtain for me plenitude of all virtues and perfection—*one Our Father, three Hail Marys.*

- O holy Archangels, obtain for me conformity to the will of God—*one Our Father, three Hail Marys.*

- O holy angels, O faithful guardian angels, obtain for me true humility and great confidence in the divine mercy—*one Our Father, three Hail Marys.*

CREDITS AND PERMISSIONS

Saint Michael the Archangel

Color Plate. St. Michael confounding the Devil by Raphael. Louvre, Paris. Photo Credit: Scala/Art Resource, NY.

Prayer to St. Michael. Public Domain. Originally appeared as "Prayer to St. Michael" in *Raccolta:1910 Edition*, Section 292.

Saint Michael Prayer (Shortened Version). Courtesy of Musica Sacra (www.musicasacra.com). Originally appeared as "St. Michael Prayer (Shortened Version)" in *1962 Missale Romanum*. All rights reserved. Used by permission. (Church Music Association of America, Richmond, VA).

Prayer for Help against Spiritual Enemies. Courtesy of TAN Books and St. Benedict Press. Originally appeared as "Prayer for Help against Spiritual Enemies" in *St. Michael and the Angels: A Month with St. Michael and the Holy Angels* compiled by approved sources (TAN Books, Charlotte, NC, 1993).

Novena for St. Michael. Courtesy of Saint Michael's Call (www.saint-mike.org). Originally appeared as "Novena for St. Michael" at www.saint-mike.org/library/novenas/stmichael.html. (St. Michael's Call, Ottumwa, IA).

Litany of St. Michael. Courtesy of TAN Books and St. Benedict Press. Originally appeared as "Litany of St. Michael" in *St. Michael and the Angels: A Month with St. Michael and the Holy Angels* compiled by approved sources (TAN Books, Charlotte, NC, 1993).

The Chaplet of St. Michael. Public Domain. Originally appeared as "The Chaplet of St. Michael" in *Raccolta:1910 Edition*, Section 291.

Saint Gabriel the Archangel

Color Plate. Annunciation by Alessandro Allori. Accademia, Florence, Italy. Photo Credit: Scala/Art Resource, NY.

Prayer to St. Gabriel for Intercession. Courtesy of TAN Books and St. Benedict Press. Originally appeared as "Prayer to St. Gabriel for Intercession" in *St. Michael and the Angels: A Month with St. Michael and the Holy Angels* compiled by approved sources (TAN Books, Charlotte, NC, 1993).

Prayer to St. Gabriel for Others. Courtesy of TAN Books and St. Benedict Press. Originally appeared as "Prayer to St. Gabriel for Others" in *St. Michael and the Angels: A Month with St. Michael and the Holy Angels* compiled by approved sources (TAN Books, Charlotte, NC, 1993).

Novena Prayer to St. Gabriel. Public Domain. Appeared as "Novena Prayer to Saint Gabriel" on www.sarahsarchangels.com.

Litany of St. Gabriel. Courtesy of TAN Books and St. Benedict Press. Originally appeared as "Litany of St. Gabriel" in *St. Michael and the Angels: A Month with St. Michael and the Holy Angels* compiled by approved sources (TAN Books, Charlotte, NC, 1993).

Chaplet of St. Gabriel. Courtesy of Patricia S. Quintiliani and St. Benedict Abbey. © Patricia S. Quintiliani. Originally appeared as "Chaplet of St. Gabriel" in *My Treasury of Chaplets: 7th Edition* by Patricia S. Quintiliani (Ravengate Press, Still River, MA, 1999).

Saint Raphael the Archangel

Color Plate. Tobias Taking Leave of His Father by William-Adolphe Bourguereau. Hermitage, St. Petersburg, Russa. Photo Credit: Scala/Art Resource, NY.

Prayer to St. Raphael the Archangel. Public Domain. Originally appeared as "Prayer to St. Raphael the Archangel" in *Raccolta:1910 Edition*, Section 295.

Prayer to St. Raphael for a Happy Meeting. Courtesy of TAN Books and St. Benedict Press. Originally appeared as "Prayer to St. Raphael for a Happy Meeting" in *St. Michael and the Angels: A Month with St. Michael and the Holy Angels* compiled by approved sources (TAN Books, Charlotte, NC, 1993).

Novena to St. Raphael. Courtesy of TAN Books and St. Benedict Press. Originally appeared as "Novena to St. Raphael" in *St. Michael and the Angels: A Month with St. Michael and the Holy Angels* compiled by approved sources (TAN Books, Charlotte, NC, 1993).

Litany of St. Raphael. Courtesy of TAN Books and St. Benedict Press. Originally appeared as "Litany of St. Raphael" in *St. Michael and the Angels: A Month with St. Michael and the Holy Angels* compiled by approved sources (TAN Books, Charlotte, NC, 1993).

Chaplet of St. Raphael. Courtesy of Patricia S. Quintiliani and St. Benedict Abbey. © Patricia S. Quintiliani. Originally appeared as "Chaplet of St. Raphael" in *My Treasury of Chaplets: 7th Edition* by Patricia S. Quintiliani (Ravengate Press, Still River, MA, 1999).

Our Guardian Angel

Color Plate. The Guardian Angel by Pietro da Cortona. Galleria Nazionale d'Arte Antica, Rome, Italty. Photo Credit: Scala/Ministero per i Beni e la Attività culturali/Art Resource, NY.

Guardian Angel Prayer. Public Domain. Originally appeared as "Guardian Angel Prayer" in *Raccolta:1910 Edition*, Section 296.

Memorare to Our Guardian Angel. Courtesy of TAN Books and St. Benedict Press. Originally appeared as "Memorare to Our Guardian Angel" in *St. Michael and the Angels: A Month with St. Michael and the Holy Angels* compiled by approved sources (TAN Books, Charlotte, NC, 1993).

St. Gertrude's Guardian Angel Prayer. Courtesy of TAN Books and St. Benedict Press. Originally appeared as "St. Gertrude's Guardian Angel Prayer" in *St. Michael and the Angels: A Month with St. Michael and the Holy Angels* compiled by approved sources (TAN Books, Charlotte, NC, 1993).

Recommendation to One's Guardian Angel for a Happy Hour of Death. Courtesy of TAN Books and St. Benedict Press. Originally appeared as "Recommendation to One's Guardian Angel for a Happy Hour of Death" in *St. Michael and the Angels: A Month with St. Michael and the Holy Angels* compiled by approved sources (TAN Books, Charlotte, NC, 1993).

Aspiration to Our Guardian Angel. Courtesy of TAN Books and St. Benedict Press. Originally appeared as "Aspiration to Our Guardian Angel." in *St. Michael and the Angels: A Month with St. Michael and the Holy Angels* compiled by approved sources (TAN Books, Charlotte, NC, 1993).

Novena to Our Guardian Angel. Courtesy of Catholic Doors Ministry (www.catholicdoors.com). Originally appeared as "Novena to Our Guardian Angel" at www.catholicdoors.com/prayers/english2/p00850.htm (Catholic Doors Ministry, Saskatoon, SK, Canada).

Litany to the Guardian Angel. Courtesy of TAN Books and St. Benedict Press. Originally appeared as "Litany to the Guardian Angel." in *St. Michael and the Angels: A Month with St. Michael and the Holy Angels* compiled by approved sources (TAN Books, Charlotte, NC, 1993).

Chaplet of the Holy Angels. Public Domain. Appeared as "Chaplet of the Holy Angels" on www.viarosa.com/VR/Angels/Guardian.html.

CATHOLIC DEVOTIONALS

A Catholic Prayer Companion. A reverent presentation of thirty of the most popular Catholic prayers. 30-minute CD, $12.95; also available as a 48-page booklet, $4.95; large print edition, $5.95

Scriptural Meditations for the Divine Mercy Chaplet, Franciscan Crown, Seven Sorrows, and the Rosary. Four popular Catholic devotions accompanied by a short passage from Scripture to inspire meditation. 80-page booklet, $6.95

Rosary Novenas to Our Lady. The classic "little blue book" with directions and prayers for making the Rosary Novenas to Our Lady, now updated to include the Mysteries of Light. 48-page booklet, $4.95; large print edition, $5.95

The Rosary: Including the Mysteries of Light. Includes brief scriptural reflections before each decade and original musical accompaniment. 92-minute double CD, $14.95

The Pray-Along Rosary. A shorter version of the Rosary for those who have limited time. Each set of mysteries runs only about 15 minutes. 64-minute CD $12.95

The Treasury of Catholic Devotions. Includes the Pray-Along Rosary, the Stations of the Cross, Litanies with Music, and Novenas with Music. 135-minute double CD, $19.95

Lentan Devotions. Includes the Stations of the Cross and the Seven Last Words. 105-minute double CD, $14.95

Available from booksellers or call 800-397-2282
www.actapublications.com